tributaries

Volume 78

Sun Tracks
An American Indian Literary Series

Series Editor
Ofelia Zepeda

Editorial Committee
Larry Evers
Joy Harjo
Geary Hobson
N. Scott Momaday
Irvin Morris
Simon J. Ortiz
Craig Santos Perez
Kate Shanley
Leslie Marmon Silko
Luci Tapahonso

tributaries

Laura Da'

THE UNIVERSITY OF
ARIZONA PRESS

TUCSON

The University of Arizona Press
www.uapress.arizona.edu

Printed in the United States of America
20 19 18 17 16 15   6 5 4 3 2 1

ISBN-13: 978-0-8165-3155-4 (paper)

Cover designed by Leigh McDonald
Cover art by Jarrod Da'

Publication of this book is made possible in part by the proceeds of a permanent endowment created with the assistance of a Challenge Grant from the National Endowment for the Humanities, a federal agency.

Library of Congress Cataloging-in-Publication Data
Da, Laura, author.
 Tributaries / Laura Da.
    pages cm — (Sun tracks : an American Indian literary series ; v. 78)
  Summary: "This poetry manuscript combines lyrical, historical, personal, and narrative poetry. The narrative scope of the manuscript moves from the period of Indian Removal in the 1830s through the period of Allotment and the Dawes Act of the 1900s and into the present"— Provided by publisher.
  Includes bibliographical references.
  ISBN 978-0-8165-3155-4 (pbk. : alk. paper)
  1. American poetry—Indian authors. I. Title. II. Series: Sun tracks ; v. 78.
  PS501.S85 vol. 78
  [PS3604.A16]
  811'.6—dc23
                              2014030795

♾ This paper meets the requirements of ANSI/NISO Z39.48-1992 (Permanence of Paper).

CONTENTS

ACKNOWLEDGMENTS

Grateful acknowledgment is made to the editors of the following publications in which these poems appeared:

The Tecumseh Motel in *Effigies II*, Salt Press, 2014: "A Mighty Pulverizing Machine," "American Towns," "Basement Storage at the Museum of the American Indian," "Five Songs for Lazarus Shale," "Hived Bees in Winter," "Measuring the Distance to Oklahoma," "No Longer," "Raven Talks Curriculum," "Spring Thaw and the Land Runs," "The Tecumseh Motel," "Vantage," "Wars of Attrition"
American Indian Culture and Research Journal: "Della," "The Indian School Graduates," "Lazarus Riding Home," "Raven Talks Curriculum," "Spring Thaw and the Land Runs," "Winter Dance of the Oldest Child"
Borderline: "Advice to an Indian Agent"
Codex: "The Haskell Marching Band," "Passive Voice"
Drunken Boat: "Measuring the Distance to Oklahoma"
First Intensity: "Baselining," "Basement Storage at the Museum of the American Indian"
Hanging Loose: "Five Songs for Lazarus Shale," "The Tecumseh Motel," "Vantage"
The Iowa Review: "The Butterfly Effect," "The Myth of the West"
Mudlark: "A Mighty Pulverizing Machine," "American Towns," "Poor Lazarus"
Prairie Schooner: "Hived Bees in Winter," "Irreversibility," "No Longer," "Wars of Attrition"
Raven Chronicles: "Earth Mover"
Red Ink: "Audubon and the Shawnee Swans"

tributaries

THE ALWAYS FRONTIER

Earth Mover

Ferocious and sly, my mind's talon
plucks liquid movements from rivers,

arteries, ink, amniotic fluid, delicate webs of optical nerves.
Puckered prospect of the Cesarean veil.

My skin twisted in stainless steel pliers proves
the efficacy of the spinal block that dulls

my pain but leaves a cavity for the sonic panic
of my child heaved from my abdomen.

I close my eyes and roll hills,
churn rivers, press shovel to earth and brace

for the abrasion that draws the past
glistening into the present.

In the Ohio Valley, mound builders
left massive earthworks.

Enamored with the idea of excavation,
settlers pilfered through the soil,

sorted remnants: feather headdresses, flakes of mica, pot shards,
bone fragments. When asked to define

an effigy depicted in a perplexing mound—
the Shawnee described *a perilous being wrought*

like a massive panther swimming
through rivers with the power to destroy

and renew. Alligator Mound.
No. I net the past and future in panther skin.

My son's ferocious cry—fanged and clawed
grip on the skin of the toppling world.

I clamp down on the tributary's gush,
lay claim to our place here.

Raven Talks Curriculum

1.

Raven curls his talons
against the newspaper rag
of a seventh grade textbook
that attributes his myth
to an anthropologist
who traveled along the Pacific Coast
fifty years ago
recording tribal creation stories.

2.

In fifth grade, I rode the bus
to the local museum on a school field trip.

The river was splitting its banks,
creeping up the margins of the road.
Mottled stones
with the patchy lichen-skin
and bulky silhouettes
of kids slumped on a couch
were disappearing
under the murky slush of flood water.
Bright pink flash of molting leaves
glimpsed through the bus window
hinted at salmon in the eddy.

At the museum, I was unhinged by old bounty signs
from the fur wars
offering the largest pile of gold for men's scalps,
less for women,
a token amount for children and infants.
I traced my finger over the name Snoqualmie, unbelieving.

Listening to the curator read aloud from the myth of raven,
I counted on my fingers
back ten years at a time to 1860
until the teacher jerked them away into my lap
and snapped my attention to the front.

3.

Fifty years ago,
the five most likely
themes employed to describe
Native Americans in textbooks:
Noble Savage
Warrior
Chief
Protestor
White Man's Helper

2013: the school district procures
new texts—feigned Native narratives.
As if to say with a shrug,
colonialism had children and grandchildren too.
In the end, even the stories are acquisitions.

        Who is this trickster
sauntering receding coasts
scattering light and darkness?

4.

Heavy thud of the book
slamming shut
pinions Raven into a bentwood box of pulp
where dark seeps out of the feathery ink of the font.

The students shade the standardized test
in fine, soft strokes of graphite—fish-scale dents
on the show-and-tell arrowhead.

Basement Storage at the Museum of the American Indian

Down here humidity
serpentines and leaves pale crescents
on the sides of pots stacked at eye level.
Like saltwater crusting on a stack of shark fins.

After the thump and click of the doors locking behind us,
I resist the urge to panic.
The fluorescent light panels cast an amniotic blue
across the fingered ridges of the platters on the bottom shelves.

A comb has been dragged through these rows and held tight.
Can a connection be drawn to the children swapped at birth?

Someone whispers slowly that
it is a graveyard down here.

Visible discomfort spreads throughout the room
and a woman shakes her head.
She wants to get home in time for the five o'clock news
which will profile a special
on children swapped at birth.

In the corner a pile of axes are stacked
relics from the first time
one was thrown over a shoulder
to mine for this museum.

The results were disastrous:
busted bentwood boxes and fractions of Anasazi polychrome.

Now those shattered pieces
have been strapped with sinew
or glued and reglued in lines
like split lips and wet strands of hair.

A side cabinet is jerked out on oiled hinges
and beaded leggings sit, tagged with plastic
in static-resistant tissue paper.
The curator mumbles
distinctly Plains
and two people bicker about the Comanche influence
in northern New Mexico.

The ticks of vents punctuate
cadences in the voice of the guard
who speaks with her back
to a shelf of Pojoaque red ware
and her arm draped across a coiled pot.

She pulls a chip of tile into her hands
blows the dust off
and returns it to its shelf.

The Tecumseh Motel

In Shawnee cosmology,
a shooting star can fall to earth as a mythical panther.

>   Tecumseh—
>   phonetic approximation of an Algonquian name:
>   Shooting Star,
>   One Who Waits,
>   Crouching Panther.

The first cultural event in Chillicothe
is a matinee performance
of an outdoor play
highlighting Tecumseh's life.
We are honored guests,
ushered backstage before the show.

How to approximate a scalping at the Tecumseh Outdoor Drama:
>   Hollow an egg with care.
>   Fill with Karo syrup and red tempera paint.
>   Soak a toupee with cherry Kool-Aid and mineral oil.
>   Crack the egg onto the actor's head.
>   Red matter will slide down the crown
>   and eggshell will mimic shards of skull.

Actors on horseback frame the stage.
A roan flicks his tail irritably at flies
as his rider shifts uncertainly on the saddle blanket.

How to approximate death by gauntlet:
>   The victim must lead the action.
>   The aggressor follows.
>   Burn marks are approximated on the actor's chest
>   with burnt ends of wine corks
>   hidden in the sand at his feet.
>   The knife is dull edged,
>   lined with a small tubing mechanism.
>   The actor squeezes a pump
>   of corn syrup, liquid soap, and red food dye
>   in a limp arc across the torso.

At the end of the performance
the crowd turns a standing ovation
to the representatives of our tribe
sitting in the middle rows.
Are we mocked or honored with such a display?
That evening,
I rail glibly on the telephone:
      historical inaccuracies,
           hooping and hollering,
                  pandering to the worst stereotypes.
My husband interrupts me—
    You sound like you've been crying.

A Chillicothe chief to the British Army Commander in 1779:
    We have always been the frontier.

American Towns

Seneca, Missouri—soft wash of casino jangle
seeps through the Pontiac's cracked window.

The map flutters on the dashboard,
one corner grit-soaked.

Sparse Ozark wash of tawny green.
A herd of buffalo lowing in the side pasture.

Here is the voyage,
conjured homeland to conjured homeland.

No, not that clawed trajectory of the past,
but a fierce conception

that quickens and scrapes inside just the same.
The drive to Ohio will take

eleven hours and forty-eight minutes,
cost one hundred and ninety-five dollars in gas.

Chillicothe—in the subtle semantics
of Shawnee, a tightened fist of connotation:

clan name and principal city,
all human systems working in harmony.

Limpid sashay of corn tassels along the byway.
Historical markers beckon the reader

to plunge an arm into the loam
tweeze with fingers to feel how fecund,

no rocks to bend the ploughshare.
What heirloom fields of Shawnee

corn hum under the crust
beside the carbon of burned council houses?

August wheeze of Bad Axe Creek.
Drought thrusts large boulders jutting up waist-high,

deep grooves in the center
for grinding corn. What is owed

grits in the corners of the mouth.
The plaque on the museum's door in Xenia extols

a Revolutionary War hero:
The ground on which this council house stands is unstained

with blood and is pure as my heart which wishes
for nothing so much as peace and brotherly love.

Summer school kids mill around the museum.
The teacher introduces the panel of tribal council members

as *remnants of the once great Shawnee tribe.*
Listless murmur of pencils across paper.

In the front room, a volunteer curator leans over a diorama
anxious to capture the real story

of a Revolutionary War camp.
He stipples red paint onto the sandy ground

simulating the gore of a military flogging,
points with the paintbrush to the next room

where fifty-three letters from 1783 broker captive trades
with the Delaware and Shawnee:

wan shades of ink from blanched olive to cornflower,
blotted in the rough or refined sway of long dead hands

each one made phylum by the promise of whiskey.
Leaving Xenia that evening on an old Shawnee trade route

retraced in concrete: Monlutha's Town, Wapakoneta,
Blue Jacket's Town, Mackachack, Wapotomica.

Xenia—the influence of the pollen
upon the form of the fruit.

I want my ink to bellow—
Where is this ground unstained with blood?

LAZARUS SHALE:
THE PERIOD OF REMOVAL

Five Songs for Lazarus Shale

> It gives me pleasure to announce to Congress that
> the benevolent policy of the Government, steadily
> pursued for nearly thirty years, in relation to the
> removal of the Indians beyond the white settlement
> is approaching to a happy consummation.
> —PRESIDENT ANDREW JACKSON, 1830

1.

There was a word for village
that meant all at once:
perfect home
perfect man
all human systems working in harmony.
A Shawnee village was a good genius society.
Names were to be guarded.

First memory:
clambering onto a horse
toes splayed for purchase
peering over the swayed back
at a curving glimmer of tributaries.
Listing rows of corn as far as the eyes could travel.

2.

Running on spindly legs
and speaking in a bubbling rush of Shawnee
the boy fled through cane breaks
when the Indian Agent called.

A child's arrow tipped with a gar's fin
pointed to the eddy.

In the wilted moon,
the Quakers gave him the name.
Bible held hovering out of reach
as he grasped at the inked picture
of a man shouldering out of a stone tomb.

The agent sat in the back pew, sniffing the end of a quill,
a slim flask of ink between his knees.
Wet trail of letters on the ledger: Lazarus Shale.

3.

Tawny coffee beans, bolts of calico, molasses,
rations passed out the back door.
Speculation at the trading post
on the topic of removal:
Lewistown first, then Lima village
Hog Creek on down the curve of the river to Wapakoneta.

Sap moon cold.
Traders walking foundered horses over coals
anticipating army requisitions.

Lazarus tracing letters in the ash,
his aunt stitching rounded meadow flowers onto doe skin:
pumpkin yellow, greasy blue and green, white-heart red beads.
The baby waking every so often to press a few grains into her chubby
fingertips.
Tallow flicker across their mother.

Why, Sister, you're beading in the old style.

In the rafters,
her fingers turning back to unbraiding.
The family's dried corn falling in dusty ropes.

4.

Journeying cake.

In the morning,
Quakers pressed wrapped suppers into their hands,
reading from the Book of Ruth over the noise of the muster.

Generic native ash-cake baked in an open fire.

Dig under the crust to find the varieties of corn
in the charred fields of Wapakoneta:
dent
flint
Boone County White
Bloody Butcher

*Journeying cake Shawnee cake or every man's cake becoming jonny or johnny
cake.*

Walking away, south along the Scioto
looking back often.
Vivid shoots of green corn
rippling along the trail in a delicate commotion.
Fingers bent against the leather satchel
pinching at grains of corn bread.
Lazarus, who else could tell this story?

5.

In Shawnee tradition
one is cautioned to cross a river
quickly, without looking down
to tempt swift creatures
ready to rend the body in riparian embrace.
Underwater panthers.
Left to ponder such beings,
the mind balks.
Mad River.
Scioto.
Great and Little Miami.

Shawnee translations of the rivers of Wapakoneta.
Auglaize River: the falling timbers on the river.
Blanchard's Ford of the Auglaize: claws in the water.

Hived Bees in Winter

> The Indians (as yesterday) remained
> as quiet as hived bees in the winter.
> Daniel R. Dunihue, Superintendent of Indian
> Removal, "Journal of Occurrences," 1832

1.

Plum moon heat—deep and pungent.
The Wapakoneta band of Shawnee
muster in a grove to wait for four days' rations.

In the periphery,
the horizon is a memory palace.
A verse is woven
into the curve of the river.
Hiding in a fringed prairie opening
is an account
of the maiden
who fell in love with the loon.

Driven slowly into the west,
the old folks walk cowed
bending low into the corn.

Three men petition for permission to make camp
beside hunched burial mounds
along the Scioto.

The superintendent of Indian affairs acquiesces:
I did intend going tonight to the feast of the Indians.
Death feast.

Upon leaving the graves,
an orator laments.
It is their custom to recite
and mutually and undisquietly
express their sorrow for their losses.

The superintendent is startled awake
by a stray horse trailing a rawhide hobble.
The heat is gentle yet.
A line of women are sitting on the wagon and chanting;
under their draped legs are sleeping children.

In the miles that follow,
a singer prods the corners of his mouth
scanning the horizon for a forgotten refrain.

2.

South of Fort Wayne,
wilted moon
sweats the Maumee River.
A woman wakes the camp
shaking and clattering her arms together.
Wet cough like a bare foot sucked out of deep mud.

Young ones
scour the fields for corncobs
lingering after the harvest.
Their bones recognize the chill is different,
punctuated one night by a prairie fire
wafting on tall grass and crackling to the east.
Waxed comb dragged through hair,
heavy with the smell of bear grease and honey.
Crackle and snap as lice and eggs are lathed
onto a whetstone and flicked into the fire.

The horses scrape lichen from tree trunks,
grow surly and thin,
foundered in trail sludge.

Lazarus is lolling along the back of one.
Palms down on its shaggy neck
to soak up the warmth.

The superintendent calls a halt
at the intersection
of the St. Joseph, St. Marys, and the Maumee
and ponders the flooded rivers
from early morning to mid-afternoon.

Militia men place bets
and aim at a sleeping turtle on the opposite bank.

Fording in the early evening,
they cross through razed cornfields
and march down the portage road
to the Wabash Agency.

Gawkers spread around.
Shivering in the muddy space between
the quartermaster's shack
and the kitchen garden.

A man in a waxed brown cape
darts in and out of the crowd
flashing a flask and sloshing whiskey in a bottle.
Lazarus buries his face into his cousin's tunic.
With two fingers, the man twists his chin back out
into the gloaming.

3.

December's moon is eccentric,
January's severe.
Clean geometry of trumpeter swans stitching
a slab of sky.

Snuffling bear
on the edge of the encampment
nosing for a cache of acorns.

Lazarus has been chewing the horses' oats,
nibbling the trampled grass,
dusty tang of urine and hint of molasses on his molars.

The flock of swans
lights down and,
in their churning multitude,
they melt a frozen pond to sleet.
Giddy with hunger, he grasps at their necks,
knee deep in icy water.

In the early dawn,
small imp,
Lazarus crouches beside an old man.
Seated on a tree branch
downwind of the hunt so they must squint to see.

The hunter hides in a hollow log with a leg of rancid deer,
drawing the bear deeper and deeper in.
Another man squats above, waiting at the knothole
to drive an arrow deep into the bear's head.

Sated, Lazarus rubs oil into his hair
shakes his limbs, huffing like a bear in the snow.
Pausing dizzy as he hears a hollow whicker.
The mare's time has come.

Creekside, groaning softly as her knees buckle.
White pills of lather
foam in the pockets of her flanks.

The foal slips neatly in an envelope of mucus
and the mare turns
to nip the cord and consume the waxy placenta.

A man aprons a ration of oats,
strokes the mare's neck in circular motions
and beckons to Lazarus.

Run your hands all over the colt. Trace every part of him.
Lazarus, he'll always be fond of your touch.

4.

At the waxing of the crow moon,
the most skilled midwife died coughing.

They are in open prairie,
no fluttering branches
or creek bank caress.
So the girl whimpers in the corner of the tent
and turns her face into its dank scent.

Women pull her closer to the brazier.
Her dress rucks up around her hips,
sharp lavender tributaries of veins
standing out across her thighs and belly.
This is her first, so she writhes when she should rest
and begs for her mother in fitful starts.

Fingers dipped in grease move nimbly between her legs.
She is cajoled
oiled slick,
cradled and lullabied.
In frustration, one woman slaps her hands together
and speaks sternly to her.

When she finally tears, the babies seem to hurtle out,
one on the other's heels.
She reclines on her elbows
as the women caress
their small mouths to her nipples.

The people sit around the fire.
Children are allowed to stay up
and meagerly gorge
on strips of dried venison, bear and swan
in honor of the propitious birth of twins.
       Mama, what is he saying?

Lazarus is lolling with his back
against his Mama's legs as the head man drones on.

He reminds us
in the old times
babble of the smallest children
was most auspicious.

Bread Dancing in Indian Territory

1.

Lazarus Shale has a bet riding
that he can make his uncle's foundered sorrel
whole before the bread dance.

He cures the horse
over a greenwood fire,
twitching him still
with a hemp lariat
and massaging his charred hooves
with pitchy resin and ash.

Riding home to the Salt Flats,
Lazarus finds himself
amidst a herd of antelope.
Urging the gelding to a brisk trot,
he reckons at least a quarter of an hour having passed
before he is free of the herd.

He eats a smoky saddle of antelope at noon,
catches a snake
of such prodigious length
its rattle sizes up to his fist.

At the edge of the encampment
he kicks the horse into a showy gallop,
dismounts whooping.
> *You owe me uncle, pay up.*

The ball game starts as the air cools.
All the young men and women face off,
the last splash of sun like a cracked egg
sliding down their foreheads.
Lazarus grins at his little sister.
Lithe brown bodies careen—no score is kept.
As the night draws in, the Shawnee gather
and what follows
is closed to us.

2.

Spring burst and crows
gather at the banks of the flooded Kaw—
noise of timbers snapping in the water
   caw, caw, caw, caw.

The mill splinters.
Cholera spread by settlers passing
through the Oregon Trail
seeps.

Riding down to the mission
on a spirited little buckskin
green-broke for the Indian Agent,
it pangs Lazarus
to let the animal go.
So he slows to a trot
a mile from town,
lights unnecessarily
from the horse's back
and cradles his hooves
checking for phantom burrs and stones.

When he ties the horse to the hitching post
the agent writes him a letter of sale,
holds it back for a minute.
There is no record of a Shale child at the mission school.
  And how old, Lazarus, is that sister of yours?

3.

Lazarus' sister is wandering the bluffs
of a swollen creek
a few miles into the prairie and holding
a picture of bright purple
coneflowers in her mind.
       Elk root.
Kneeling at the aster flash
of lavender amidst the dun
and digging a funnel to the roots,
she tosses the heavy stems onto the flat bed
of the donkey cart.

Homeward,
the wheel creak startles her mother from the straw pallet
where she shivers and sweats in turns.

Auntie Shale opens the cabin door.
       You stay on that path
       niece, don't come in and wake your Mama.

Judy Shale, long legs in a pinafore
many years outgrown
twirls the donkey's ears,
whisks flies from his pale muzzle.

She's bound—
for the fields
where the young ones who are able
collect buffalo bones to sell for fertilizer.

       How's my Mama faring?
She stalls, eyes slanting to the space inside the door.
       I'm hungry, Auntie.
Judy catches the boiled egg,
lobbed high into the air,
in the billow of her apron.
The donkey shies lazily in his stays.

On the road, she leaves:
the elk root wrapped in dry grass,
a pyramid of five corn cakes
embossed with the slim print of her thumb,
and a soft trail of eggshell
dusting the ground in her wake.

4.

The siblings ride double to the mission.
Lazarus signs the ledger,
fingers wrapped around the quill
like gripping a rattlesnake fang.
          Rations for the Destitute Shawnee.

He reaches back reflexively to steady the burden.
Judy's slight weight replaced by
the wool, lard, sacks of cornmeal.

Later that winter,
an issue of the *Shawnee Sun* newspaper,
          Siwinowe Kisibwi,
is disseminated to benefactors on the East Coast.
Ladies of the tea societies murmur
over the visual cacophony of Shawnee—
a feisty child's first scribbles.

They ponder a portrait
of a beautiful indigenous adolescent.
Round, dark eyes,
downy cross hatching across the cheeks
to hint at the blood blooming
beneath her ochre skin.

The Good Genius Society

An exhibition of the new mill is held in early summer.
Finally finished, straddling a slim tributary of the Kaw,

it oozes grain and lures families down from the Salt Flats.
Blanket Indians encouraged onto the mission

with the promise of milled corn and flour rations,
salt pork, yellow coffee beans, calico, glass beads, their children,

almost free from the mission school.
But first the recital of verses, the mock table

laid with care for the visiting missionaries and charity representatives.
All along the walls of the meeting house, schoolwork is on display.

Pinafores stitched from old mattress ticking.
Lumpy ploughshares from the boys' foundry.

Slates are lined up on the wainscoting. A reckoning
of tribal stories: The woman who fell in love with the loon.

An account of the panther and the swan.
The myths of the good genius society.

Judy Shale reads a story aloud to her Auntie and Mama
in measured tones—great turtle of the earth,

the swan pulling the southern people
from the saltwater to the back of the panther.

Lazarus hangs back unsure
if they are honored or mocked with such a display.

Advice to an Indian Agent

Advice to a young Indian Agent:
>   *This country will not cradle the eye.*
Lope through a buffalo wallow
with only your head
lolling above ground like a specter.
Flickering swish of your mare's chestnut tail.

Note the map:
Indian Territory—no less than six times the breadth
of Ohio, and who can say we failed
to provide for these souls
in anything less than a Christian manner?

Do not neglect your letters to the missionary ladies' tea societies.

You cannot imagine how hard
it is to juice a bit of knowledge
from these people. First,
you must know
that an Indian baby is named
for his clan
which is generally some wild beast.

Take this new boy
from the mission school,
pushing a broom in the corner.
Now, this child was born to the panther clan
in late winter
when it is assumed that every animal is starving.
So you see, there is the reference to the beast
and the moon of the boy's birth.
As the child grows, so too the name.
If swift, he could become Running Panther,
If thoughtful, Panther in Winter.

Alone, the new Agent
pulls a finger of whiskey slowly into his mouth—
firm amber handshake
and turns aside as if addressing a friend.
>   *No cradles for the fucking eye.*

Across the threshold stands
the boy's father
come down to the agency from the Salt Flats
with a string of broke horses to sell.
Clatter of the broom
as the boy
darts out the door and into his arms
to be swung chuckling onto a yearling's back.
That boy is Starving Panther.

>   *When will the boy's name change?*
The Agent hollers from the mission stoop.
The father levels a cool stare.
>   *His name is William.*

Poor Lazarus

Live long enough
and salt pork, beans,
yearling colts, honey and butter,
        something will turn into a wedge
        to bend your will.

Missionaries call for my sons to send off to school,
each season when the corn is green.
I tuck them into the rows
farthest to the north of my cabin.
Keep them busy with the threshing as I whisper
their true names into the ears we consume,
        but I leave a path to them
        like a snake
        by slithering away through the sparse harvest.

Frost breaks under my mare's hooves
when I ride to sign my name at the Neosho mission.
My sons and nephews
traded to industrial school in the north
        for the release of seven barrels of winter rations.

This commerce—
makes me brother to dragons, companion to owls.

Riding away from the mission,
I call to my sister's youngest child,
        the only one
        still too young for school,
        Come over here and ride with your old uncle.

The boy clambers up behind me,
bare toe notched into the girth for warmth and purchase.
My boots quiver along the sides of the horse's flanks
        as I endeavor to slip them into the stirrups
        that frame the ground below in jerky patches.

Child, I keep repeating, *Nephew.*
The horse dances nervously,
sensing my frenzy.
To his credit,
        the boy
        keeps a steady hand on the reins.

Lazarus Riding Home

Skin for skin
my senses know
       the lanky, liver chestnut
       canter-song
             scattering pebbles
in front of my cabin

and before I see
the Indian Agent from Neosho
looming beside my corn

my ears wince.

Old panic
       to have such a man in my sight,
       carrying his trade in saddlebags:
       full burlap sack of tobacco
       and calico to barter
       for my compliance.
       Singed smell of the vinegar and smoke
           he uses as a screen from Indian dirt.

Miami, Seneca, Shawnee and Wyandotte—
head men from each tribe are singled out
in a vulture-slow loop,

       beckoned into town
       to stand—silent as field stones
       to greet the fearsome Modoc.
       A new tribe
       exiled from the West
       and punished like us
       onto this land that our feet still mistrust.

We ride to Baxter Station,
busy with city folks, ranchers,
soldiers, Indian agents, gawkers.

A newspaper man
jots notes on a grimy fistful
of paste cards.

Waxy-still cattle cars straddle the tracks.
Deep in the corners, an arm
slithers through the creosote-soaked slats.
            A child's dark eye
            meets mine
            through a knothole.

My sorrel starts under me
as I dismount.
A young soldier
hauls an axe
            and chips ineffectively
            at the chain
            that holds the cattle car doors together
            in a crooked embrace.

The agent preens for the crowd,
his starched collar growing dusky.

Behold the fearsome Modoc.
That chain snaking down to the ground like a panther's howl.
A scattering of men
            dressed in prison stripes and leather
            are bound at the wrists
            and watered from buckets held up to their chins.

The youngest soldier, red-faced,
points his rifle to the ground
and swallows hard. A Modoc boy
holds his sister and swings his legs
on the station ledge
            kneecaps massive against his slender limbs.

I was that child's age
when I walked
    from Ohio
    to Indian Territory.
    Eighteen months
    with my arms rucked up around my baby sister
    and my eyes locked on my Mama's shoulders,
    harried by soldiers and agents.
    So many times I heard them call
    If you slow us down
    swear to God you are not worth bullets.
After fifty years, this is what it tastes like: thistles for wheat
at the root of my tongue.

The Modoc boy turns his sister's chin into his tunic,
covering her eyes
and I draw stares as I haul my body up into the saddle to leave.
    Sometimes I need
    my mare under me
    to share the weight.

Having grown old in that meager shelter
    of shadows cast by horses.

Indian Territory, November 1873.

LAZARUS' CHILDREN: SEVERALTY

A Mighty Pulverizing Machine

To each orphaned child—so long as you remain close enough to walk to your living kin you will dance, feast, feel community in food. This cannot stand. Eighty acres allotted.

To each head of household—so long as you remember your tribal words for village you will recollect that the grasses still grow and the rivers still flow. So long as you teach your children these words they will remember as well. This we cannot allow. One hundred and sixty acres allotted.

To each elder unable to till or hunt—so long as your old and injurious habits sing out over the drum or flicker near the fire you cripple our reward. We seek to hasten your end. Eighty acres allotted.

To each widowed wife—so long as you can make your mark, your land may be leased. A blessing on your mark when you sign it and walk closer to your favored white sister. Eighty acres allotted.

To each full blood—so long as you have an open hand, we shall fill it with a broken ploughshare. One hundred and sixty acres allotted.

To each half blood, each quarter strain—so long as you yearn for the broken ploughshare, you will be provided a spade honed to razor in its place. When every acre of your allotment has been leased or sold, you will turn it on yourself. From that date begins our real and permanent progress.

Winter Dance of the Oldest Child

1.

First light.
The oldest girl patches cracks in the wall
with sacking soaked
in potato starch.

Long strips of burlap
freeze solid
before she can work them
soft with the tips
of her fingers. Hint
of ice-shard light and smell
of last summer's harvest rot wafting
from the stacked cornstalks
insulating the cabin's western wall.

She papers the walls
with old newspapers from last year's missionary basket:
American Agriculturist, Colman's Rural World, Prairie Farmer.
Advertisements stare her down
all through winter's tallow light:
threshers, ploughshares,
leather martingales to tamp the necks of
draft horses into more pleasing lines.

On the table—pale green and amber beads
creep up unfinished moccasins
in a woven pattern of geometric corn shafts.

Her granny sleeps
under an unfinished morning-star quilt
still in piece work,
baste stitched.

2.

Drowsing on the milk stool,
the little brown Guernsey's soft eyes soothing
then piss-heavy tail
whipping her into reality.

Blunt cries of the baby
lowing through the cabin door
while her thumb and pointer finger
pinch into the warm milk,
dripping the heat down her throat in a shamed rush.

Her baby brother roots desperately at her
new breasts
through the calico warp of the apron—pain so bright and urgent
she thinks her body's been peeled from its skin.
She bites a whimper for their mother off
at the root of her tongue
as she trails a creamy snake of milk
down the channel of her pinkie finger
into the baby's mouth, crooning.

Whimpering and wide eyed, her brother
is like a green-broke colt, shying at the sound
of icicles splintering off the branches
and dimpling the ground outside.
Until, soothed by the milk,
his features wrap and tuck
into a mask of self-satisfaction
as he settles
into the straw.

And for the first time since waking,
the girl lets her body
settle for a moment too,
seeing milk, eggs, a finger of molasses, even some flour
on the table.

3.

Winnowing afternoon light
plucks at the zigzag line
of spring-green seed beads
running up the seam of the leather moccasin.

The girl pauses momentarily
to cut the wick,
lick her needle,
dip her wet fingertip in the beads
and hold it studded in the light—
the beads like a cluster of pin headed beetles.

She's waiting for her father to ride home
with the start of the month rations.
Perhaps the preacher is
making the most of his captive audience
waiting out the back of the mission church.
The wicker baskets of salt pork
and coffee sitting in rows
just inside their line of sight.

But she worries
as the sky darkens
and she strains her ears against the quiet,
fatigued by the absence of hoofbeats.
Her worry becomes a dancing
honey finger of whiskey in her mind.

She flicks the beads from her finger
and huffs out to the coop
breaking an old hen's neck
with a breathless
snap over her shoulder.

Fries the bird, crackle of the skin on her tongue
the warmest thing she's felt in weeks.

Spring Thaw and the Land Runs

Zinc mining wives
traipse through the muck,
black leather toes
like picks. The station market in Neosho is a little reward
waved before them by prospecting husbands
to ease the burden of being a territorial spouse.
The exotic spread across the tines of the railroad tracks.

Women selling blankets
drape them across the hitching posts
for the settlers who come in waves.

A Shawnee girl places her beaded
moccasins on a bed of corn husks.
When she stands,
her baby brother
clings to her collar,
splays his bare toes
against her instep and shins
trying to crawl back up into her arms.
He dangles there unwilling
to put his feet back onto the ground.

The mining wives cluck
at the growing crowd of sooners,
offer the girl half price for a tiny set of moccasins,
not bothering to smile at the baby's antics.

The next season turns the prairie.

Ochre-threshing of the unassigned land runs:
Sac and Fox,
          Pottawatomie,
                    Iowa,
                              Shawnee.

Della

What I remember of my life
the season before
I was sent to school:
I rose every morning on the beach
of our summer grounds, pushed aside
a veil of butter yellow deer hide—
lake water so vast
it bowed across my sight
         startled me awake.

I learned with my milk teeth
to suck the sweetness from wild rice hulls.

I was just old enough
to trail behind my older cousins
berry picking.
They argued over who would
carry me over each hill,
it was a matter of pride
between them
that my feet—bare or wrapped
in bear cub skin—
rarely touched the ground.
They praised the soft thumps of
my berries in the wicker basket.

That winter I was shipped
across the flat lands.
My eyes filled
with dishwater.
My feet no longer swept
off the ground.

For the next ten years
just when winter was breaking into spring
I would glimpse the Sandhill Cranes
tuck and lift in flight

from the ponds out behind Haskell Indian School.
They paused so briefly before flying north and home
on that sparse water
that gaped across the prairieland.
         Bullet holes in a deerskin racked too thin.

The Haskell Marching Band

In the basement of Haskell Indian School,
she was one of the girls standing assembly style
pressing flour into pie tins.

Long hours at the school's foundry made him crepuscular.
Accustomed to seeing his shadow in waxy pre-dawn light,
he would pause near the basement bakery's vent,
warmth blossoming around his ankles as he placed his boots in the slush
and stomped out a tune that she'd recognize
from the last night's band rehearsal.

After graduation, they married:
the band had to find
another trumpeter—
the quartet a new flutist.

Thirteen summers of work release—
eighteen-hour days and humid hayloft nights
allowed him to buy his trumpet from the music instructor.
The flute stayed behind.

The Indian School Graduates

They sit out back of the boardinghouse,
tin plates across their knees.
Scratchy smell of linoleum tacked to creosote.
Through the door
they catch a crescent
      glimpse into the kitchen
      of sausages on waxed paper drawing flies.

He crumples a handbill lauding new statehood
and promising cattle work
in New Mexico,
      jots a quick map in the dust with his boot heel
      and signs it **Shale** with a twig.

She pokes warily at the mutton stew
spiced with green chili
that brings bile up her throat
      and makes her baby batter and kick
      inside the taut skin of her distended belly.

An old man shuffles out of the boardinghouse,
his silhouette lurching in the starlight.
He sits and pares at a wound
with a pocketknife
groans and holds a spent bullet
in his tobacco-stained fingers and
      flits a line of blood
      across the bucket of peeled potatoes.

He twists his finger up
at the almond sliver of moon,
freckled splatter of the Pleiades
then back at the couple.
He points with his lips south to the foothills.
      With no clear intention of smiling
      his teeth force his mouth into a half grin.

They wake under what the locals
call the tortilla stars,
and light out into the west.

Irreversibility

> The significance of the dam is not found alone
> in the magnitude of its dimensions, nor in the
> workmanship that has gone into its construction. It
> lies rather in the ends which are to be served.
> —L. IKES, SECRETARY, UNITED STATES DEPARTMENT
> OF THE INTERIOR, 1947

Balanced on an iron trellis
over the Columbia River
a recollection of massive sturgeon
dappling under the glassy surface waves
like sunken panthers.
     Coulee Dam
     Bonneville
     Richland

When a family immigrates
what trails in its wake?
Irrigation's slick hope seeps
into the shady corners of company towns,
entropy unspools:
     Cle Elum
     Diablo
     Conconully

The oldest girl watches
workers shoveling concrete and shale into a gulley.
Fearing rattlesnakes, she terrifies her siblings
by pointing out glinting chips of mica and proclaiming them fangs.
     Priest Rapids
     Lower Monumental
     Mud Mountain
     Ice Harbor
     Granite

What swims stunted rivers
whimpering and scratching
for riparian embrace?
Recollect—before the dam, salmon in the river swam so thickly
they could be speared from horseback.

Audubon and the Shawnee Swans

> Imagine, Reader, that a flock of fifty Swans are
> sporting before you, as they have more than once
> been in my sight, and you will feel as I have felt,
> more happy and void of care than I can describe.
> —JOHN JAMES AUDUBON

Slaughter a flock of birds.

Still the rustling chaos of feathers and talons.

The recollecting mind stumbles into an aviary—
      feathers flutter into the air
      birdsong fragments sail.

      Memento Mori in dusty folios:
      Carolina Parakeet
      Passenger Pigeon
      Labrador Duck
      Great Auk

On a belated honeymoon
canoeing up the Ohio River
Audubon chanced upon fifty Shawnee Indians

and five hundred swans
churning the sleet of a small pond
to liquid.

Audubon noted in his journal:
      an account of a Shawnee bear hunt—
the hunter crouching in a log
drawing the bear deeper and deeper in,

an auspicious birth of twins.

If they lived on:
        Carolina Parakeet
        Passenger Pigeon
        Labrador Duck
        Great Auk
songs would mark the movements of their lives.
Cascades of swan feathers
and the birdsong of endless flight
stamped into the whorls of their ears.

To the Shawnee,
        the babble of very small children
        was the language of the infinite.

Audubon was known to destroy his paintings
to motivate himself to greater artistic excellence.

Imagine him
plucking feathers
to strip and fold into a leather journal.
Frantically sketching

the swan decomposing against the locust tree—
ferocious wind ripping through the tent's canvas sides
        transformed into a tableau—
        balmy spring, lily pads
        the slender neck and bright eye approximated on canvas.

The mind can grasp the swan.

But not trumpeting of fifty in an icy pond.
Not a murmur of the mother struggling in labor
what her twins howled out or who listened.

NO LONGER

No Longer

Removal—that sorrow trail
　　　　but a weary exile just the same.

What tremor can be measured
in the pale wave of light
　　　　that blazes a path of eviction?

Gazing at maps,
water calls attention through absence.
Lakes and river reaches
in Northeastern Oklahoma,
　　　　the Scioto, Rio Grande, Kaw
　　　　　　　　Columbia and Snoqualmie.

Watery seduction—
　　　　migration's
　　　　　　　　sultry stroke of fatigue.

To visualize the stones of a dry riverbed—
　　　　stubble of a razed cornfield—
　　　　　　　　cultivate the ankle's gaze.

To weather that expulsion path—
　　　　hunch the shoulders into a perpetual wince.
Look back often.
Squint in the light
that shines on the backs of the knees.

Conceive a vista:
deliver hills sleek
　　　　as a panther's shoulder blades.

Finger a rattlesnake fang
drag its miniature scimitar
through river clay
　　　　inscribe the clans
　　　　of a good genius
　　　　　　　　society.

Measuring the Distance to Oklahoma

Shell shaking in the state of the coin toss and sorrowful walk.

Weaving through the powwow grounds
grass stomped low and buzzing with flies
      your son walks two quick steps ahead of me
      to point out a tiny bow and arrow at a vendor's booth.

Rats scuttle in the grain silo.
The gentle clamor of the casino washes through the parking lot.
A table is piled with half a dozen corn cakes,
each one embossed with the maker's thumbprint.
Your grandfather recounts
catching water moccasins as a boy
and spitting wads of tobacco down their throats
just to watch them squirm.

You sink onto a dusty quilt
gently pull the empty Coke can from your boy's sleeping fist
shake your head impatiently when your daughter whines for you to
untie an intricately beaded belt from her regalia.
Child's arrow, capped with a pencil eraser twirling in your fingers.

Ottawa County moon as seen from a distance:
pale vodka swirling in an open mouth.
Driving home on the frontage road,
green and riveted as a turtle's back.
Highway sketched into place by the broken black lines
of oil rigs at midnight.

Baselining

In a hospital waiting room in Santa Fe, New Mexico,
a man's boot heel poised over a woman's fingers
melting into the paisley carpet.
Two doors down, a wax thermometer melts in a fevered mouth.
Flavors of the month:
syrupy insulin in the blood, sodium heparin soaking the kidneys.
He is cursing her mouth: a rusty pair of scissors and tongue, a sharpened
chisel.
The walls will never recover from this match
says a woman pounding her fist on the table.
She sings a song as they drag a scalpel across the curve of her abdomen.
Things to remember:
shining lights on the backs of your knees prevents jet lag,
children who draw pictures without legs or feet are in need of support,
it's called baselining.
There are noble gasses in every hospital waiting room.
A frog can ease your pain.
There are noble gasses in every hospital waiting room.

The Butterfly Effect

Tonight the moon is full
and seems to remember

when she pulled her torso
from the penny slot machine

at Santa Ana Casino.
Parallel tracks in arroyo dust

unfurl rivers in La Plata county.
The doorknob is island sand

in the fingers. A monarch
flaps its wings, polar caps sheathe ice,

the tides creep forward.
The Pleiades throw down

a peninsula of shadow,
I reach for the almond sliver

of Orion's belt.
A moth's wings tear

a patch through rainfall.
The hinged rhythm of sleep;

speed and chrysalis as wind scissoring
across the withers of a racehorse.

The Myth of the West

On the frigid side of a mountain
a fern unfurls.
        A man on horseback picks through a clear-cut.

A sudden storm
weaves a net of stimulation.
Off an island coast
a gray shark's embryo sinks.

This velvet subversion;
a diver walks backwards into the tide
and listens from his heels
as the ocean hums
in the flat blue language
of the computer screen.

Drought radiates from a sidewalk's whorled spine.
Ocean salt scours an inland parking lot.
Freeways jangle their spurs
across the routes of the west.

One day
a fractured skull may break free
of the anthropologist's saline myth.
A glacial wind will pull the names
from the water tower's hunched shoulders.

Ninety-seven horses
paw out of fingerlights
        of dappled ground.

Raven Gets Meta

Raven's marking time in the public school system.
On the first day of instruction he forgets the syllabus,

improvises, tells the class a story about himself.
How, in his younger days, he was one of the many

who helped to stipple the night sky with light. Believe it,
or don't. Many others presumed

to use the stars
to cast connect-the-dot sketches of their own likenesses

onto that endlessly beckoning blackboard,
but he threw his lights

in a five-minutes-left-of-recess-heads-up frenzy.
Raven prefers his constellations wild

and that leads to tonight's homework:
Sneak out of your beds.

Walk barefoot outside.
Look up. Raven smirks at the orange chairs left pushed out.

Mid-semester, the administration calls Raven to the carpet
for a certain cavalier attitude

toward the test-prep curriculum. He slinks late
into the meeting, feathers rustling

at the Power Point projected on the bare west wall
assessing average reading scores

and annual measurable objectives.
Echoes come in from down the hall:

See the world in a grain of sand from the English classroom
and the science lab's

butterfly flicker moving polar ice.
Raven's been around the block, has wrapped his talons

around stones so large
they made the cosmos.

Raven doesn't give a shit
about his students making adequate yearly progress

on any standardized test.
But when asked to imagine seeing any one child contained

in the pixelated dot flickering on the bar graph
dancing across the projection screen,

a shrill caw
spirals up the length of him.

These tricksters.
Looking into galaxies and yearning for self-portraits.

Sixth Grade

Leaning in
to hear a recorded sample
of a sixth-grade student
reading haltingly
from a script of Rip Van Winkle,

I see a child,
arms stretched
mid-yawn
acting out the part of
Rip as he wakes
supine
from his long sleep
in the woods.

Five of the children
acting as villagers in the background
wear airbrushed shirts
commemorating deceased relatives.

A girl pouring
bright colors of tempera paint
into paper Dixie cups
winces when pigment
bleeds together on her backdrop.

A bright hair molts
from my scalp
and falls diagonally
across the keyboard.

Sometimes my sleep is interrupted
by dreams of urgent hands
waving in the air,
students slanting
frantically in their desks
floating beyond
my peripheral vision.

Passive Voice

I use a trick to teach students
how to avoid passive voice.

Circle the verbs.
Imagine inserting "by zombies"
after each one.

Have the words been claimed
by the flesh-hungry undead?
If so, passive voice.

I wonder if these
sixth graders will recollect,
on summer vacation,
as they stretch their legs
on the way home
from Yellowstone or Yosemite
and the byway's historical marker
beckons them to the
site of an Indian village—

Where *trouble was brewing.*
Where, *after further hostilities, the army was directed to enter.*
Where *the village was razed after the skirmish occurred.*
Where *most were women and children.*

Riveted bramble of passive verbs
etched in wood—
stripped hands
breaking up from the dry ground
to pinch the meat
of their young red tongues.

Wars of Attrition

Mapping out territory
in 1984—
        my older cousin
            ditched me
in the scrub brush behind our granny's house

locked in a dog crate, five years old,
            howling.

Nine years ago, I taught her oldest child
how to write her name
on the back of a grocery list.

        My hand huge over her crayon
        clamped fist.

Paper plastered across her boxy little torso
like a peace treaty
        as she galloped through the living room.

I was teaching seventh grade when my cousin died,
sugar gumming up her system
        like a glinting trail of dried snot.

Unable to focus,
        my mind
            flitted over the Cascades
            past a lake full of tree trunks
            poking up like rotten molars

landed in Eastern Washington
            next to my grandmother's backyard—
            next to my cousin's red curls.

A map is not a neutral document,
        one of my students parroted
        bubble eyed.

And I muttered
        that's right
            correct.

Vantage

Driving past Vantage:
>damp sign proclaiming ginkgo fossils

and iron sculpture of wild horses on the ridge.

At the turn of the last century,
Cayuse ponies were bred with European draft horses.
>A leaner, tougher work animal for the logging fields.

Trumpeter swans stitch
>the sallow slab of sky.
>>Two birds swap point position
>>to cut the air's polarity.

Path that pulls the taste
of mixed blood into my mouth.
Late February
and I am three weeks pregnant. I drive
>and the Columbia loosens
>>my dad's easy silence.

He talks about his grandfather:
star musician of the Haskell Indian School Marching Band,
>telegraph operator, rodeo cowboy?

Tracking his family across
three states to hunt for big game
was habitual.

My grandfather,
dead within a week of my birth;
>I am told
>>he looked at a Polaroid
>>and proclaimed me an angry little Indian.

Late August in a post-depression labor camp
in the Mojave desert.
>My dad was born; he might have been premature,
>>covered with dark hair and sick enough to die?

Terraced sun shower wading through the cloudbank.
        Recollection becomes embrace?

At twenty-nine weeks,
the doctor's chart advises me—
        my child is two and a half pounds, like a Chinese cabbage.

Blinking heavy eyes and fluttering his newly formed lashes.
My hair still damp from swimming laps.
        Warning signs:
                severe headaches, excessive nausea, a change in reflexes.
Feel of the doctor's hand pushing me back onto the table.

In the hospital, I ask for books.
        Posters from old rodeos.
A photo of a Mimbres pot
from southern New Mexico
black and white line figures—
        a woman dusting corn pollen over a baby's head
        during a naming ceremony.
Medieval women
        ingested apples
                with the skins incised with hymns and verses
as a portent against death in childbirth.

Heparin sodium
injected daily and nightly
        in a slow abdominal arc
incising my skin
        like a creation spiral; my hope apple.

Say splitting the rails of the body
to lay down a fence
between harm and one's young.

Terraced sun shower wading through the cloudbank.

My son at ten months
staring calmly at morning stars
during his naming.
The faint trail of corn pollen suspended
in his fine, dark hair.

I am deeply grateful to my family, friends, teachers, and students for their support and kindness. Many of these poems were written at the Institute of American Indian Arts and the Richard Hugo House, and I appreciate the advocacy and instruction both organizations have provided me and generations of other writers. The Eastern Shawnee Tribe of Oklahoma is my source of inspiration, hope, and pride. I am indebted to my tribe for much of the knowledge and impetus to create this manuscript and hope in turn that what I have written is a credit to our nation. I have been inspired and encouraged for the past ten years by my students and colleagues at Tyee Middle School, Highland Middle School, and Odle Middle School. Poets and friends who have helped me and fostered my growth as a writer include: Sherman Alexie, Sherwin Bitsui, Allison Hedge Coke, Jon Davis, Tara Hardy, Mischele Jamgochian, and Arthur Sze. "Vantage" is dedicated to my son Tony.

NOTES

Earth Mover

Alligator Mound is an effigy mound in Granville, Ohio. It depicts a four legged creature with a long, curling tail.

American Towns

Seneca is a small town in Missouri that borders the Eastern Shawnee Reservation. Xenia and Chillicothe are both towns in Ohio that cover historical Shawnee villages.

Five Songs for Lazarus Shale and Hived Bees in Winter

"Journeying cake" is a reference to the linguistic variation of names for corn bread.

A "Journal of Occurrences" was required by the government as a document of Indian Removal. The journal of occurrences cited in "Five Songs for Lazarus Shale" and "Hived Bees in Winter" was maintained by Daniel Dunihue during the removal of the Seneca and Shawnee from Ohio to Indian Territory. Dunihue was appointed by his cousin, James B. Gardiner, to help conduct the removal. Gardener negotiated the Lewiston and Wapaghkonnetta treaties that led to the removal of the Shawnee from Ohio.

"The Indians (as yesterday) remained as quiet as hived bees in the winter."

—Daniel R. Dunihue, Superintendent of Indian Removal

"Journal of Occurrences," 1832

Dunihue made this entry the Sunday before the caravan of Shawnee Removal started from Ohio.

"Wilted moon," "sap moon," "plum moon," "eccentric moon," "crow moon," and "severe moon" are all translations of Shawnee moons.

Lewiston, Hog Creek, Wapakoneta, and Lima are all traditional villages in Ohio from which the Shawnee were removed during the period of Indian Removal.

Dent, flint, Boone County White, Bloody Butcher—these are all varieties of corn.

The translations of the Shawnee names for rivers are from the papers of Col. John Johnson. Johnson was an Indian Agent for nearly fifty years before and during the period of Indian Removal.

Bread Dancing in Indian Territory

Siwinowe Kisibwi, the Shawnee Sun newspaper, was composed entirely in Shawnee and was the first of its kind in the United States. It was produced in 1835.

Kaw Flood—The Kaw River flooded in 1844. Few records were made of the outcome of the flood as it primarily impacted indigenous people.

Poor Lazarus

Neosho Indian Agent—Indian Territory was split into agencies. The Eastern Shawnee tribe reported to the Neosho agency.

Lazarus Riding Home

Modoc Removal—after the Modoc War of 1872 and 1873, the Modoc tribe was forcibly removed to Indian Territory. The Modoc survivors were relocated to an allotment of land next to that of the Eastern Shawnee Tribe.

Vinegar and Smoke—this is a reference to an Agent in Indian Territory who famously laundered his shirt in vinegar after he had any kind of contact with a Native person.

A Mighty Pulverizing Machine

President Theodore Roosevelt described the Dawes Allotment Act as "a mighty pulverizing machine intended to break up the tribal mass," in his 1889 Report to the Interior.

Winter Dance of the Oldest Child

American Agriculturist, Coleman's Rural World, Prairie Farmer—missionary baskets often contained outdated periodicals to encourage Natives to embrace the agrarian lifestyle.

Spring Thaw and the Land Runs

Zinc Miners—the area around the Eastern Shawnee Reservation and Miami, Oklahoma, was mined for zinc from the late 1890s to the early 1910s.

In 1889 The "Homestead Act" opened the unassigned lands of Indian Territory to settlers.

Sac and Fox, Pottawatomie, Iowa, and Shawnee—these tribes were all impacted by the land runs. Collectively they lost thousands of acres of land.

The Haskell Marching Band

Haskell Indian School was established as the United States Indian Industrial Training School in 1884. A number of Shawnee children were sent to Haskell Indian School in Lawrence, Kansas. It is where my great-grandparents met.

Irreversibility

All of the listed names reference dams in Washington state.

Audubon and the Shawnee Swans

John James Audubon's journals from the early 1820s describe a chance meeting with a group of Shawnee Indians. He was invited to partake in a bear hunt, witnessed the staggering sight of a flock of more than fifty swans landing on a frozen pond, and noted the auspicious birth of twins.

Carolina Parakeet, Passenger Pigeon, Labrador Duck, and Great Auk are all American birds that Audubon noted in his diaries. These birds are now extinct.

Passive Voice

All italicized phrases are drawn from roadside markers in the western United States.

ABOUT THE AUTHOR

Laura Da' is a poet and public school teacher. A lifetime resident of the Pacific Northwest, Da' holds an AFA from the Institute of American Indian Arts, a BA from the University of Washington, and an MA from Seattle University. Da' is an enrolled member of the Eastern Shawnee Tribe of Oklahoma. She has published poems in *Prairie Schooner, Hanging Loose, The Iowa Review,* and elsewhere. Her first chapbook, *The Tecumseh Motel,* was published in *Effigies II* in 2014. She has been nominated for a Pushcart Prize and named one of Sherman Alexie's top ten Native American poets. Da' lives near Seattle with her husband and son.